CROOKED SOLEY
A CROP CIRCLE REVELATION

CROOKED SOLEY
A CROP CIRCLE REVELATION

Allan Brown & John Michell
with an afterword by PATRICK HARPUR

ROUNDHILL PRESS

Grateful acknowledgements to Patrick Harpur for his afterword, originally published in *The Cereologist*, number 1 – Summer of 1990, Steve Alexander for the use of his photographs, Una Woodruff for elements used in diagram on page 61 and John Martineau for invaluable help with diagrams & for teaching me techniques he developed at Wooden Books.

For further help and and information, thanks are due to Richard Adams, Mark Carol, Polly Carson, Nigel Coke, Michael 'O'Conner, Dave Godwin, Emma Holmwood, Peter Howard, Christine Rhone, Elizabeth Rosson, Andy Thomas & Colm Tohill.

Thank you to Michael Glickman for encouragement, support and friendship.

Special thanks to Alex, Annette, Iain, Michelle & Lucy Brown; Colin & Joan Harding.

Thanks to the whole croppy fraternity for excitement, inspiration, hoaxes, rumours, disinformation, good humour and excellent company.

Dedicated to Alex, Darroch, Isla & Oonagh

First Published in 2005 by Roundhill Press,
2a Crescent Road,
Brighton,
East Sussex,
BN2 3RP

Copyright © Allan Brown & John Michell 2005.

ISBN 0-9549855-0-8

A CIP catalogue record for this book is available from the British Library.

Book design & illustrations by Allan Brown @ Roundhill Press.

Photography by Steve Alexander.

Printed by Antony Rowe Ltd,
Bumper's Farm Ind Est,
Bristol Road,
Chippenham,
Wiltshire
SN14 6LH

List of contents

"Straight trees have crooked roots."
Anonymous, 16th century

The straight and the crooked

"Prepare a way for the Lord;
  clear a straight path for him.
  Every valley shall be filled,
  and every mountain and hill shall be brought low;
  and the crooked shall be made straight,
  and the rough ways shall be made smooth,
  and all mankind shall see God's deliverance."
  The Prophet Isaiah

"Dreamer of dreams, born out of my due time,
  Why should I strive to set the crooked straight?
  Let it suffice me that my murmuring rhyme,
  Beats with light wing against the ivory gate."
  William Morris

"If all our mental images no less than apparitions (and I see
  no reason to distinguish) are forms existing in the general vehicle
  of *Anima Mundi*, and mirrored in our particular vehicle,
  many crooked things are made straight."
  W.B. Yeats

"God is a thought who makes crooked all that is straight."
  Friedrich Nietzsche

"Straight down the crooked lane,
  And all round the square."
  Thomas Hood

Introduction:

These are remarkable times we are living in. I am constantly amazed by the revelations they are bringing forth and by the signs and wonders that come with them. But I have never been more amazed and awed that I was when Allan Brown sent me his drawings and analysis of the crop circle at Crooked Soley near Hungerford, Berkshire. This short-lived masterpiece (it lasted only a few hours before the harvesters moved in) was not only beautiful and finely crafted - as well as utterly mysterious - but it gave information, precise and numerically expressed, on a subject that I have been studying and writing about throughout my active life, the subject of ancient cosmology and the code of number on which every past civilization was founded. At the heart of this traditional code or canon are two basic components, the numbers 5040 and 7920, along with their common factor 720. These numbers were plainly emphasized in the Crooked Soley crop circle.

The circle appeared at night on 27 August 2002. It was the last major formation of the season and I was unaware of it until a year later when Allan Brown brought it to my attention. He had observed its numerical composition and recognized the significance of 5040 and 7920 through my writings about these numbers. He then waited for a year to see if anyone else would recognize them. No one did, so he wrote to me and, as said above, filled me with awe and amazement. We both agreed that a record should be made of this phenomenon, and this is it.

Here is why I am so enraptured by the apparition at Crooked Soley. Many years ago I was drawn to the study and practice of geometry. A major influence was Keith Critchlow, who founded the school of symbolic, cosmological or 'sacred' geometry that has since flourished universally. His pupils, directly or through his writings and lectures, include just about everybody with a practical, artistic or philosophical interest in the subject. Some of them are crop circle enthusiasts and, not surprisingly, they have been suspected of creating the phenomenon themselves. But I know these people - Martineau, Kollerstrom, Glickman, Brown, Schindler among them - and we all agree that none of us has the skill and originality to have designed - let alone executed - many of the magnificent, subtle, witty and highly cultured artworks that appear every summer around Avebury, Stonehenge and other ancient sanctuaries. There is a mind, and therefore a purpose, behind the crop circle phenomenon. It is an elevated mind and its purpose can be inferred from what it actually does. Crop circles bring beauty and mystery, friendships and new interests to a generation that needs them. At the same time, quietly, inoffensively, they are teaching us something. They are preparing us for something, for an event which, according to ancient records, occurs from time to time when the situation demands it - the return of the gods - the grail of knowledge and wisdom restored to earth.

That is one way of looking at it. There are many angles and approaches to the crop circle mystery, and researchers have covered most of them, but with no success at all in solving the puzzle. There seems to be no literal solution. So we are impelled towards a psychic or spiritual acceptance. Crooked Soley, it seems, represents a new stage in a process which has been going on for many years. This process was observed as early as 1959, by Carl Jung in his last and most prophetic book, *Flying Saucers*. He characterized the UFO phenomenon as a portent of radical changes in thoughts and perceptions, culminating in a renewal of divine influence - the return of the ancient gods. In crop circles, says Patrick Harpur in the afterword, Mercurius is the dominant power - the god of inspiration and learning. He is the traditional source of the revealed code of knowledge symbolized by 5040 and 7920, the numbers so beautifully encoded in the Crooked Soley formation.

John Michell

Discovery and description

The summer of 2002 was a remarkable season for crop circles. On the 15 August a striking crop formation depicting an alien holding a spiral disc with an encoded message was discovered in a wheat field on the edge of Crabwood near Winchester. It received immediate and widespread media publicity and looked certain to be the final, dramatic curtain-closer of the season. Then, out of the blue some two weeks later, in a location not previously known for crop circle activity, a masterpiece was slipped surreptitiously beneath the back door. Partly, no doubt, because of the furore created by the Crabwood Alien, it received very little attention – until later.

Everything about the Crooked Soley formation is shrouded in mystery. It was discovered only by chance, by passing pilot who alerted the crop circle photographer, Steve Alexander, to its existence. Luckily, Steve acted fast and flew over the circle without delay. He took a number of photographs just before the formation was obliterated beneath the spinning blades of the combine harvesters which can be seen, hard at work amidst clouds of dust, in the background of several of Steve's images. As far as we know, only the farmer and his son ever went into the formation, and as no ground data was ever collected, its origins have remained enigmatic.

The centre of the formation was unmarked and lay deep into the standing crop, which was intriguing, as this is where someone would have had to have stood, had the inner and outer circumferences been manually inscribed. This highlighted just one of several practical obstacles that would need to have been overcome by anyone laying out something of this complexity in the short, dark hours of a summer night. It is difficult to reproduce the design on paper, even on a small scale with the advantages of a bird's eye perspective, good lighting and freedom to rub out and correct the drawing. I have tried it several times, and so has John Michell, but we have never managed to do it without errors. Only the computer seems able to do it perfectly. It is hard to imagine how any team of surveyors could have completed the design on such a large scale – about 300 feet across – with seemingly perfect accuracy, without blunders or signs of their presence. (In fact the formation does contain a single error, one of the 'squares' that falls over a tramline is only partially flattened, as if this natural gap in the crop has confused or disrupted the continuity of the circle making process.) The real mystery to me, however, is not so much how it got there but who dreamt up this wonderful design in the first instance.

After many counts and recounts I ascertained that the pattern consisted of 144 arcs, creating a latticework field of 1296 or 6 x 6 x 6 x 6 'curved squares'- that is, 'squares' whose sides are arcs rather than straight lines. Each pair of the 144 arcs contained 17 plus two halves of these 'squares', making 18, and 18 x 72 = 1296. There are essentially just two methods of geometrically reconstructing this design and I was intrigued as to whether we could determine which had been used on the ground.

The first is a variation on a method first introduced by the beautiful Picked Hill 'Sunflower' formation of 13 August 2000 (see fig 1). In this method, each of the 44 logarithmic curves, which appear to underpin the design, are in fact composed of a series of straight lines (see fig 2).

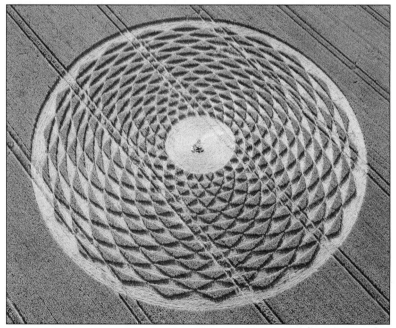

The Picked Hill 'Sunflower', Alton Barnes, Wiltshire   fig 1:

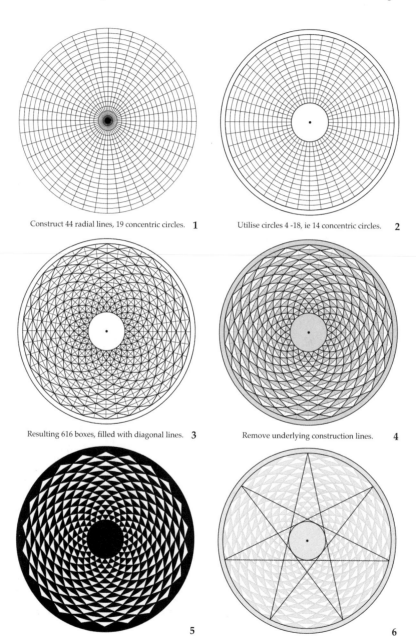

Construct 44 radial lines, 19 concentric circles. **1**

Utilise circles 4 -18, ie 14 concentric circles. **2**

Resulting 616 boxes, filled with diagonal lines. **3**

Remove underlying construction lines. **4**

5

6

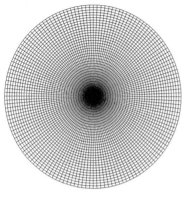

144 radial lines & 36 concentric circles.   **1**

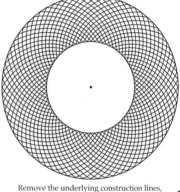

Inner 18 concentric circles
erased. 2592 boxes remain.   **2**

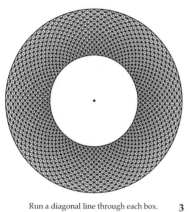

Run a diagonal line through each box.   **3**

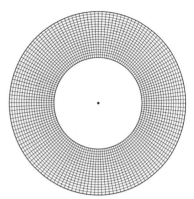

Remove the underlying construction lines,
leaving latticework field of 1296 'squares'.   **4**

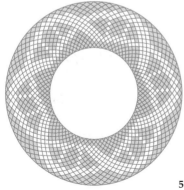

5

6

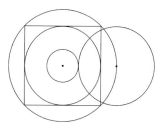

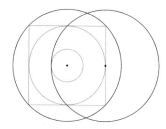

Circumscribe a circle around a square. Inscribe another circle within the square. The contained circle is displaced so that its centre sits on the circumference of original circle. A small inner circle touches the displaced sizing circle.   **1**

A circle, with its centre on the perimeter of the square, is constructed so that it touches the small inner circle.   **2**

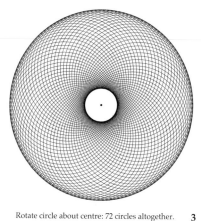

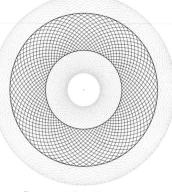

Rotate circle about centre: 72 circles altogether.   **3**

Remove superfluous lines, leaving latticework field of 1296 'squares.'   **4**

5

6

At Crooked Soley, the arcs could have been similarly created and fig 3 demonstrates how this is done. First, 144 radial lines and 36 concentric circles are plotted, the inner 18 of which are then erased, leaving a grid of 2592 boxes. Next, diagonal lines are run across each of the boxes in such a way that they create the latticework field with the prerequisite number of 'squares'.

Alternatively the design can be reconstructed in such a way that straight lines are dispensed with altogether and the 144 arcs are actually constructed from 72 circles, of which only a section is actually inscribed. This method is illustrated in fig 4, and having carefully examined all the aerial photos taken of the formation, both John and I feel sure that this was the method used.

fig 5:

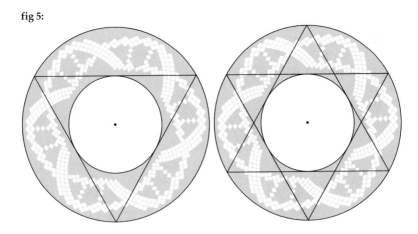

However, one of the first things I noticed when looking at the formation was that it had been constructed in such a way that an equilateral triangle, and therefore a hexagram, could be placed within the formation's outer circumference, so as to touch the central disc of standing crop contained within (see fig 5). Geometrically this tells us that the inner disc has a diameter half that of the outer circumference, even though its area would only be a quarter that of the whole. This implicit hexagonal geometry reflects the six-fold nature of both the formation's design and its inherent numerology. If the formation were constructed using the 'radial and concentric' methodology, then this particular proportion would be present as a natural artefact of construction. If the circular method were used then this equilateral arrangement would not quite work. In order to create the true proportions, both the inner and outer circumferences need to be pushed apart slightly. In fact, as John Michell describes in a later chapter, Crooked Soley appears to have been designed using a variation on the circular method, starting with the equilateral sizing proportion and then pulling the circumferences in slightly, to create the required parameters into which the design is placed. This leaves two narrow flattened bands of crop around the edges of the formation, the outer being slightly thicker than the inner. This harmonises the formation to yet another geometric order (see fig 23 and **The greater Soley circle**, page 41).

Having created a latticework field of 1296 'squares', the design is completed by flattening down a number of them, and the most amazing thing about the Crooked Soley formation is that the twisting DNA strand, with its perfect six-fold rotational symmetry was made of 792 'squares' laid down and 504 left standing. I was well acquainted with John Michell's works on ancient metrology and the sacred canon of number which he found to be at the root of all traditional cultures. These numbers 5040 and 7920 are central to this canon, and John writes about them in a following section of this book. I was staggered that these two numbers should have tumbled out of the design. How could this be?

The formation itself, irrespective of the numerology it contains, is a remarkable achievement, and although nearly three years have passed since its appearance, not a single shred of information has come to light as to who or what might have constructed it so accurately in this lonely field on the outskirts of Hungerford. The fact that it precisely and unequivocally refers to the most important numbers to have emerged through recent scholarship in sacred geometry and ancient cosmology has, as John Michell has said, all the attributes of a "divine revelation".

Prior to studying the Crooked Soley formation I could not imagine how I would have begun to fulfil a brief, in which the numbers 792 and 504 were to be coherently expressed as a graphic symbol, let alone as a perfect rotating DNA strand. Even if someone had approached me on the street and showed me the design on a piece of paper, prior to its appearance as a crop formation, I would still have been completely awestruck. This solution is so elegant that I could not believe that anyone, having conceived of and constructed it, would remain silent about it. So I sat and waited to see if someone would step forward and enlighten us to the numerology it contained. Yet in over a year, no mention was made of this vital adjunct to the design. Either the numerology thrown up by the formation was completely accidental, and had never entered the head of the designer, or we were tangibly encountering some geometrizing Platonic demiurge. Having waited for a year to see what, if anything, would emerge, I wrote to John Michell and informed him of my work on this formation.

It was not the first time that the crop circles have made reference to the DNA molecule, for back on June 17 1996 a beautiful formation was found in the famous East Field, near the tiny hamlet of Alton Barnes in Wiltshire (see fig 6).

This field was then farmed by Tim and Polly Carson who - by one of those strange coincidences that haunt this subject - had previously managed a farm at Crooked Soley, and had worked the very fields in which the Crooked Soley formation was later to appear.

The East Field 'DNA Strand', Alton Barnes, Wiltshire   fig 6:

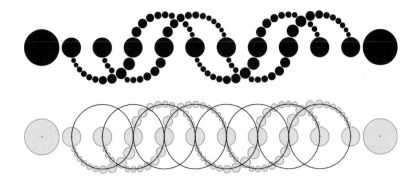

Silhouette and geometry of the East Field DNA strand fig 7:

This linear formation, 648 ft in length, symbolically depicted two polynucleotide chains in the form of a double helix spiral, with the chains open at either end, like the actual nuclear DNA molecule. As John Martineau subsequently pointed out to me, the Crooked Soley formation seems to be a depiction of mitochondrial DNA, which is the form of DNA that is passed down purely through the matriarchal line. It is distinct from the regular DNA molecule in that the open ends of the chain are linked together forming a complete loop. The mitochondrial DNA is an unbroken chain that binds us to the primordial Eve, the Goddess of All.

It is only when you try to make accurate drawings of crop circle formations that you begin to appreciate their geometric subtleties. One feature that emerged from a numerological analysis of the Crooked Soley formation was that it conveys the conventional 'pi' (π) ratio of 22/7, the ratio between the circumference of a circle and its diameter. This had previously been demonstrated in the Picked Hill 'Sunflower', of the 13 August 2000. One of the first to reproduce this design on paper was Michael Glickman. He immediately noticed the 44:14 or 22:7 pi ratio contained within the design. (The design is constructed over an underlying grid of 44 radial lines and 14 concentric rings)

There is another way in which the spiritual number 7 is expressed in the 'Sunflower'. A heptagon (7-pointed star) fits precisely within the outer circumference so as to enclose the central circular area of flattened crop (see fig 2.6).

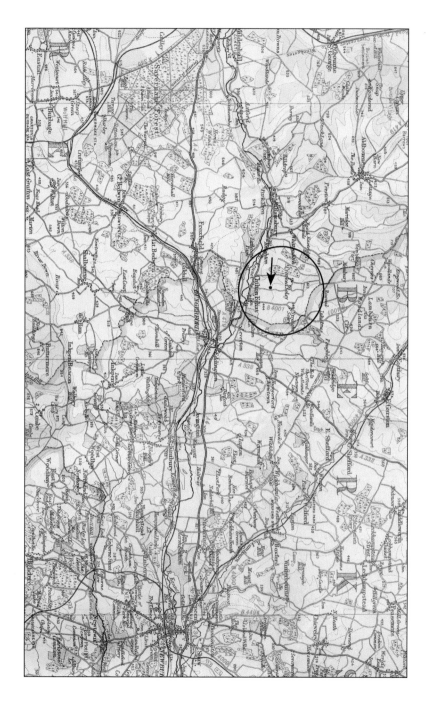

The location

We have looked at the manifest design on the ground, as well as its underlying geometry, but there is a further dimension to the Crooked Soley formation that needs to be touched on, and that is its actual location in the landscape. Crooked Soley is an odd name and although Soley is a name that has been associated with the area since the early 13th century, the Crooked prefix was added at a much later date, probably in the late 18th century. The dictionary says that Soleyn means a lonely spot or alternatively a solitary, unique wonder and both terms seem wholly appropriate to our studies. In the Middle Ages, when it consisted of open fields, Soley was a small settlement and traditionally operated under the auspices of the nearby Manor at Chilton Foliat, on the banks of the River Kennet. Only later in the 16th century were the fields enclosed and the hamlet divided into the two separate settlements of East and West Soley. By 1835 these settlements consisted of two farmsteads, East and West Soley Old Farms, and East and West Soley Farms respectively, although today only the latter three remain. In fact, to all intents and purposes the area has remained fairly unaltered since the Middle Ages and the only other noticeable changes to the landscape were the planting of the various copses. By 1791 Briary Wood and Hitchen Copse had been planted respectively east and southeast of East Soley, and in the 1880s Queen's Coppice was planted south of West Soley. The remaining copses, namely Princess Copse and King's Copse, were planted in the mid-20th century. The latter can be identified in several of Steve Alexander's photographs as the distinctive rectangular block of trees beside the formation itself (see page 10).

I visited the area some time after the event, but was unable to find any trace of where the formation had lain, but I was immediately struck by the fact that not only is there a Crooked Soley, but a Straight Soley too, and that a short footpath connects the two hamlets. I sensed immediately that this wasn't a random location choice. I was reminded of a verse by T.S. Eliot, in which he speaks in prophetic terms about the completion of an epochal cycle and the renewal of an age.

"Round and round the circle
Completing the charm
So the knot be unknotted
The cross be uncrossed
The crooked made straight
And the curse be ended"
                            T.S. Eliot

Interestingly, this very same verse had been used in the opening
article of the Winter 1991/2 edition of *The Cereologist*, the original
crop circle journal edited by John Michell (see fig 8). The verse was
run around a picture of the infamous hoaxer, Doug Bower, whose
name, weirdly, is echoed in a small copse, Bower Wood, just half a
mile northwest of Crooked Soley itself (see fig 9).

The infamous Doug Bower, as depicted in *The Cereologist*, **by Nigel Coke**   **fig 8:**

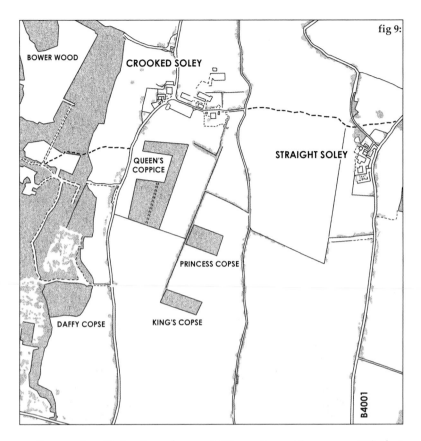

It was the distinctive shape of Kings Copse (see page 10) that enabled me to pinpoint exactly where this formation had lain, and when the site is marked on an Ordnance Survey map, it defined a specific geometric relationship with both Crooked and Straight Soley. The formation lay at exactly the same distance from Crooked Soley as it did from Straight Soley, and moreover, both Soleys lie at exactly the same distance from each other as from the formation itself (see fig 10). In other words an imaginary equilateral triangle precisely connected all three features together in the landscape.

The alchemical significance of the various names of the copses, hills and place names in this small geographic area is poignant. As well as King's Copse (Sol) and Queen's Coppice (Luna) there is a Marridge Hill (the alchemical wedding or conjunction of Sol and Luna) and if, the right-hand side of the landscape triangle is

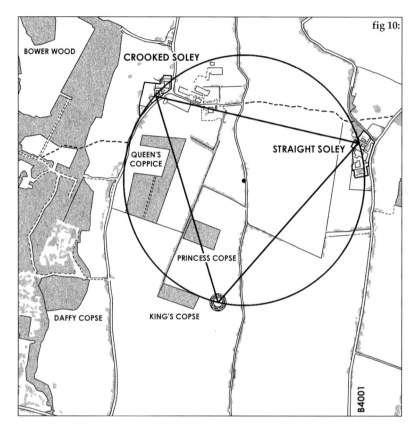

fig 10:

extended, it leads to the summit of Gold Hill (gold being the final goal of the alchemical work). The trickster Mercurius or Hermes, the winged messenger who mediates between mortals and gods, is perhaps represented by Daffy Copse, Folly Pit and Folly Farm. Etymologically the word 'Daffy' derives from an obselete 16th-century word, daff, which means to frolic or to fool, and is the root from which the word daft emerges, reflecting, perhaps, not only the folly of attempting the Great Work, but the inherent folly of crop circle research itself. The name Balaam, as in Balaam's Wood just west of Crooked Soley, reflects an old tale of mercurial inversion. Balaam, a Mesopotamian diviner, was summoned by Balak (as in the nearby Balak Farm) to curse the Israelites. God reproached Balaam, speaking through the ass he rode, sending him instead to deliver prophecies of future glories. (*Numbers 22-23*).

Another interesting dimension to this landscape work, and one that seems to perfectly reflect the daimonic nature of the event itself, is the extraordinary abundance of dualistic place names, concentrated within a two mile radius of our figure, that serve to reiterate the basic duality already established by the site of the formation, equidistant from both Crooked and Straight Soley. As well as the basic split between Crooked and Straight Soley, or West and East Soley, we have a whole series of dualities such as that between West Soley Old Farm and East Soley Old Farm and then again between West Soley Farm and East Soley Farm. Furthermore we have a King's Copse and a Queen's Coppice as well as two thin strips of woodland to the south west of Crooked Soley that serve as windbreaks called Dwarf Brake and Lower Dwarf Brake respectively. Just to the east of Straight Soley there is a New Hayward Farm and an Old Hayward Farm. Similarly there is a stretch of road nearby that has a New Hayward Bottom adjoining an Old Hayward Bottom. The large field below East Soley was called North Field and this stood opposite South Field, which lay on the other side of the River Kennett, both having been enclosed in 1813. On the corner of South Field there once existed a small lodge called East Lodge, which was mirrored a little further up stream with a West Lodge. The River Kennett itself gave rise to two marshes, an Upper and a Lower Marsh.

Just beyond the limits of this two mile radius exists a Poughley and a Lower Poughley, a Little Hidden Farm and a Great Hidden Farm, a North Hidden Farm and a South Hidden Farm, a Denford Farm and Lower Denford Farm, a Lower Slope End Farm and an Upper Slope End Farm, a Lady's Wood and a Lord's Wood, a Little West Wood and a Great West Wood, a Bonning's Copse and a Lower Bonning's Copse as well as a Starve-all Farm and a Prosperous Home Farm.

Perhaps this location was also seen as favourable because it is bounded by both the parish and the county border, which divides Wiltshire from Berkshire, thus heightening the sense that heretical events of this nature inhabit a liminal zone that lies between worlds, oscillating between the real and imagined, exactly where, Patrick Harpur reminds us, we traditionally encounter the daimonic.

Allan Brown

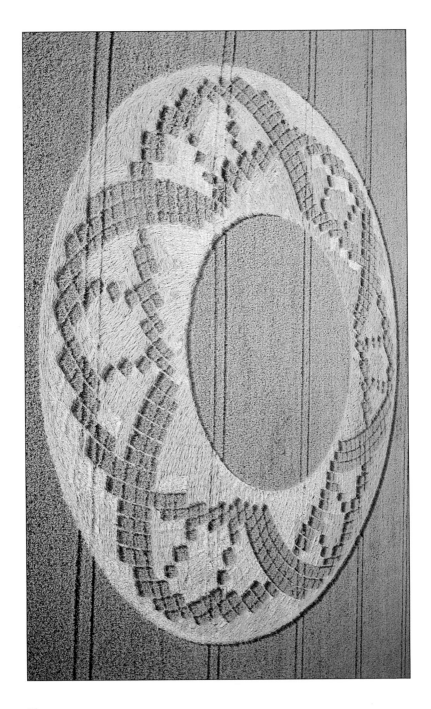

The numbers

The ultimate wonder of the Crooked Soley formation is the code of number that is displayed so beautifully in its pattern of standing and laid-down clumps of wheat. This is truly a revelation. It is either the work of an unknown, barely-imaginable genius among us or from a divine source.

5040 and 7920. Those are the numbers that stand out in the design, and with them is 720, their common factor, in terms of which they are as 7 to 11. They are neatly represented, on the scale of 1 to 10, by the 504 wheat clumps that delineate the double spiral and 792 similar areas where the crop has been laid down. The whole design was structured by 72 equal circles, centred upon 72 points spaced around the inner circle of standing wheat. Only parts of the 72 circles fall within the design area, so the result is 144 arcs, 72 in one direction and 72 in the other. Each pair of arcs encloses 18 divisions, so the whole area is of 18 x 72 = 1296 divisions. 1296 is the square of 36 and equal to 504 + 792.

These numbers, all multiplied by ten, are keys to that basic and traditional formulation of number that lay at the root of all ancient culture. In certain ages it is forgotten and society is overwhelmed by chaos. Then, in due course, it reappears, refreshing the human spirit and providing the knowledge and insight that lead to truth and justice on earth.

5040 was taken by Plato as the key symbol of the divinely ordered Creation; the 'heavenly pattern' he called it. In the perfectly civilized community that he specified in the *Laws* the number of citizens was 5040 and all its institutions were based on that number.

5040 is 1 x 2 x 3 x 4 x 5 x 6 x 7, the first seven numbers multiplied together. In arithmetic it is called 'factorial 7' and written 7! The number Seven has unique qualities that make it the natural symbol of the universal soul. Philosophers call it the Virgin and the eternal feminine in nature. On the lower plain, where numbers multiply and grow elaborate, the archetypal Seven is represented by its factorial, 5040.

The relationship of 7 and 5040 is made plain in the decad (the numbers 1 to 10 that correspond to the physical world). As seen below, 7 is the constant, unmoving pivot of the decad and provides its symmetry.

$$1 \times 2 \times 3 \times 4 \times 5 \times 6 \times 7 = 5040$$
$$7 \times 8 \times 9 \times 10 \qquad\qquad = 5040$$

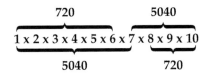

$$\underbrace{1 \times 2 \times 3 \times 4 \times 5 \times 6 \times 7 \times 8 \times 9 \times 10 \times 11}_{5040} \underbrace{}_{7920}$$

5040 was the measure that Plato gave as the radius of the city of his dreams. In his *Laws* he referred to the same scheme of cosmological geometry that St John described in his vision of the Heavenly City. Both cities are circular with radius 5040, but mysteriously they are also said to be squares. That identifies them as examples of the traditional foundation pattern in which a square and a circle were combined to imitate the marriage of eternal, spiritual values (the circle) with the earthly, practical attributes of the square.

Reconciliation of the square and the circle is geometrically achieved by drawing both figures around a common centre so that the square and the circle overlie each other and have equal perimeters. That means that the measure round the four sides of the square must be equal to the circumference of the circle. This can only be done approximately, because the measure round the square is rational, being four times its width, whereas the circle's circumference is π times its diameter, and π is an irrational number. It is, however, near enough to 22/7 for practical purposes and, with the acceptance that no description of the world can equal the real thing, that ratio is adopted in the Heavenly City diagram.

In this diagram the radius of the circle is 5040 so its circumference is 5040 x 44/7 or 31680. The square has the same measure round its four sides, so the length of one side is a fourth part of 31680, which is

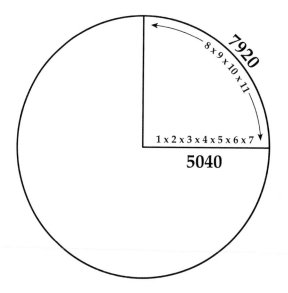

fig 11:

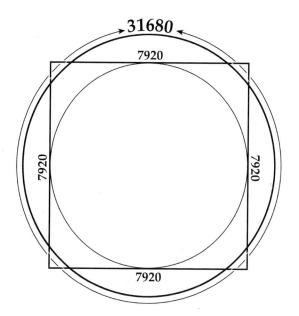

fig 12:

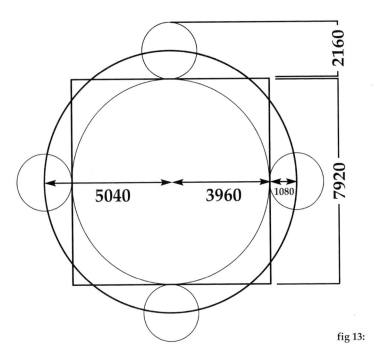

2160

7920

5040   3960   1080

fig 13:

The Great Pyramid profile from square and circle

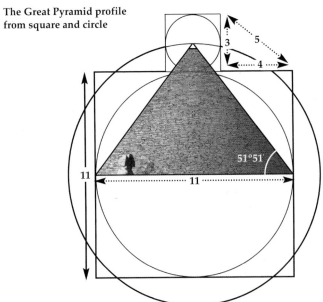

3   5

4

11   11

51°51

fig 14:

7920. That brings in the second number in the Crooked Soley circle. The third key number, 720, links 7920 to 5040 because 720 x 7 = 5040 and 720 x 11 = 7920.

These two numbers produce the 'squared circle' or circle and square with equal perimeters. The circle's radius is 5040 and the side of the square is 7920. The measure round each of those figures is the same, 31680. That was a supreme number in the mystical system of the early Christian gnostics. In formalizing the holy names of the new religion they adapted the name of its first principle, Lord Jesus Christ, so that the numerical values of the Greek letters comprising the name added up to 3168 (see pages 46-48). A tenth part of 316.8 is the number of feet in the mean circumference of the ring of lintel stones at Stonehenge, and 316.8 feet are a hundredth part of 6 miles.

Stonehenge:

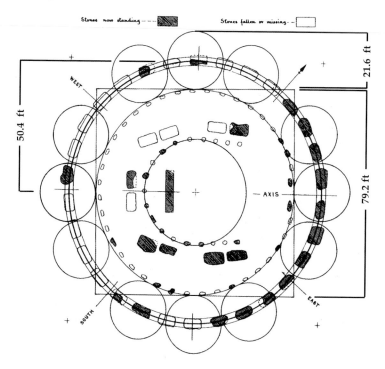

Inner bluestone circle diameter: 79.2 ft
Radius of sarsen stone circle: 50.4 ft
Circumference of sarsen stone ring: 316.8 ft

fig 15:

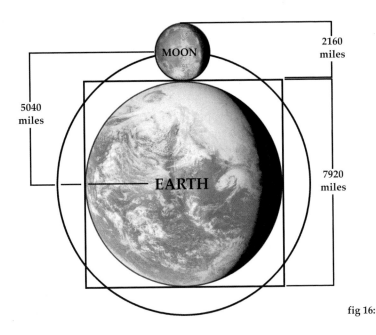

A quadrant or quarter part of a circle with radius 5040 is 7920. To find the area of a circle, the formula is to multiply the radius by half the circumference. The sum in this case is 2 x 7920 x 5040, producing the number 79,833,600, and that large number is simply twice the first eleven numbers multiplied together, or twice 1 x 2 x 3 x 4 x 5 x 6 x 7 x 8 x 9 x 10 x 11. That is because 5040 = 1 x 2 x 3 x 4 x 5 x 6 x 7, and 7920 = 8 x 9 x 10 x 11. So the area of the circle with radius 5040 is 2 x 11!

This circle which so neatly combines the numbers from 1 to 11 is of natural interest to lovers of number-play. But it is not just a curiosity, it illustrates a physical, astronomical fact, unnoticed in modern times but intensely significant to the ancients. The fact is that the respective proportions and measures of the earth and the moon are expressed in the squared circle construction produced by the numbers 5040 and 7920. The appropriate unit of measure in this and other figures of ancient cosmology is the mile of 5280 feet.

The earth's mean diameter is 7920 miles, as near as can be estimated. The moon's diameter is 2160 miles. Their respective radii are therefore 3960 and 1080 miles. The sum of these two radii is 5040. Thus, if the circle of the moon is drawn tangent to the circle of earth, and a greater circle is drawn from the centre of the earth through the centre of the moon, the radius of that circle is 5040 miles, and its circumference is 31680 miles, the same as the measure round the four sides of the square containing the earth. Thus, unnoticed by modern astronomers, the earth and moon together demonstrate the squared circle - and in the same canonical numbers that appeared in the crop circle. These numbers consist of the basic integers multiplied by 720:

$$2160 = 720 \times 3$$
$$5040 = 720 \times 7$$
$$7920 = 720 \times 11$$
$$31680 = 720 \times 44$$

This marvellous figure, alluded to in sacred writings, traditions and temple plans in every part of the ancient world, is the key to all the traditional sciences. It accommodates in its framework all systems of geometry, number and measure. Expressed in it are the canons of sacred music, the cycles of chronology and the harmonies of planetary motion. At various times over thousands of years, ideal constitutions have been created on the model of this cosmological figure. It is like the Holy Grail which, whenever it appears, brings light and knowledge into human affairs. And here it is again, this divine instrument of happiness on earth, not discovered and proclaimed by learned professors, but briefly and mysteriously depicted in a remote cornfield. This the mark of a refined culture, higher than anything we are familiar with today.

First published in 1972 (John Michell - *City of Revelation*), the twelve-faceted diagram that develops from the circle squared by earth and moon is known to students of ancient cosmology as the Heavenly City plan. It represents the 'sublunary world' - the realm of earth under the influence of the moon. This is the most interesting part of the universe, as far as we are concerned, but it is not the whole. The deficiency is indicated by the incomplete numerical composition of the Heavenly City plan. The area of its circle is, as shown above, twice 11! But the area of the Universal Circle should be six times greater, or 12! (the first twelve numbers multiplied together in recognition of the twelve gods of classical cosmogony). The geometry of that greater circle and its relationship to the Heavenly City on earth is shown in the following diagrams.

Construction sequence of the Universal Circle

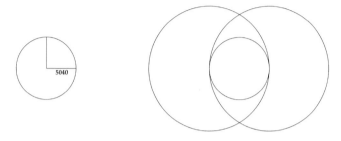

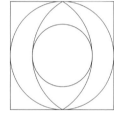

Circle: radius 5040. **1**

Construct vesica pisces around circle. **2**

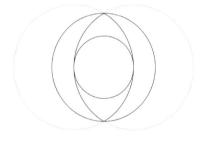

Enclose the vesica pisces in a circle. **3**

Enclose in a square. **4**

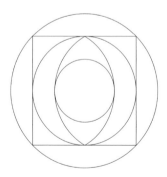

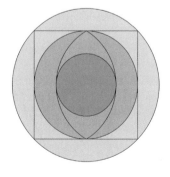

A containing circle completes the construction. **5**

The 3 circles highlighted. **6**

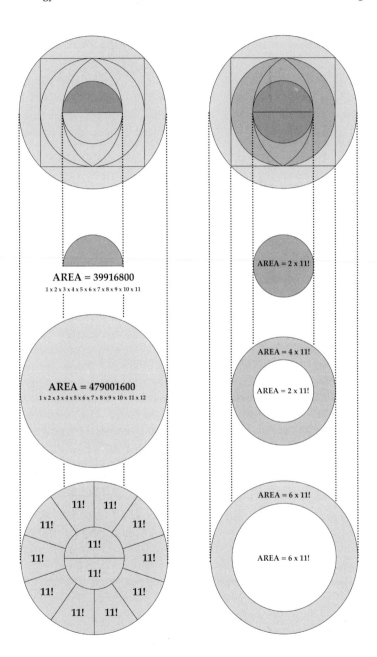

AREA = 39916800
1 x 2 x 3 x 4 x 5 x 6 x 7 x 8 x 9 x 10 x 11

AREA = 2 x 11!

AREA = 4 x 11!

AREA = 479001600
1 x 2 x 3 x 4 x 5 x 6 x 7 x 8 x 9 x 10 x 11 x 12

AREA = 2 x 11!

AREA = 6 x 11!

11! 11!
11!   11!
11!
11!   11!
11!
11!   11!
11!   11!

AREA = 6 x 11!

The process is simple, but it provides a complete course in symbolic geometry, introducing in order the figures and ratios by which, according to the traditional creation myth, the world was made. These are:

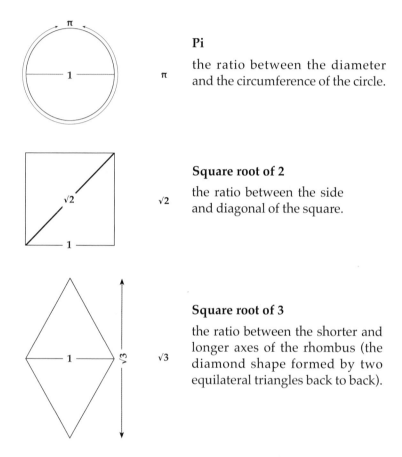

Pi

π

the ratio between the diameter and the circumference of the circle.

Square root of 2

√2

the ratio between the side and diagonal of the square.

Square root of 3

√3

the ratio between the shorter and longer axes of the rhombus (the diamond shape formed by two equilateral triangles back to back).

These ratios provide the links between the Universal Circle with area of 12! and the circle of the sublunary world with radius of 7! On this level appears a further ratio, the square root of 5 which generates the famous 'golden section' of 1 : 1.618... (phi ø). This ratio lies behind the spirals of plant growth and the proportions of life generally. It is symbolic of nature and humanity. In contrast, the number 6 with its inorganic, repetitive geometry typifies the crystalline structure of inanimate nature, minerals, rocks and water.

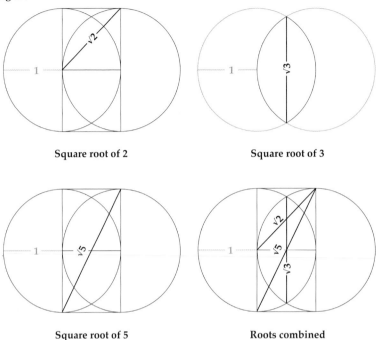

Square root of 2   Square root of 3

Square root of 5   Roots combined

Most prominent in the Heavenly City diagram are the numbers 12 and 7. They represent opposite principles, Twelve being the number of order and reason and Seven standing for inspiration and the irrational element. The qualities of Seven have been touched upon earlier. It is the number of the World Soul, the supreme goddess who existed before Creation. Twelve is the master number, dominating the field of Number itself. It structures the circle of the Zodiac, measure, sacred music and the cycles of time. It gave form to ancient civilizations with their 12 gods, tribes, rulers and social divisions. In the traditional city plan, Twelve provided the apparent framework, but at the centre of all was the Oracle, a manifestation of the number Seven. Decisions were made by the twelve city elders, but they were then referred to the oracle, the soul and conscience of the community, and if she rejected them they were abandoned. The model for these societies was the Heavenly City plan, in which the 12-part overall design accommodates the geometry of Seven, throughout and at its centre.

The circle divided into 28 parts to produce a square with the same perimeter as the circle

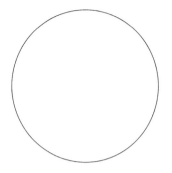

Inscribe a circle.

1

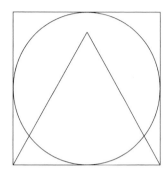

Enclose circle in a square & construct equilateral triangle on base of square.

2

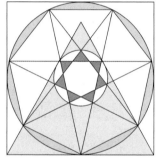

Construct a heptagram using intersection points of circle and triangle. A further heptagon is neatly held within the triangle.

3

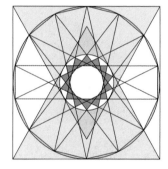

Second, draw a reciprocal triangle on the opposite side of square.

4

Two further triangles complete the division of circle into 28 parts.
(error 1:0.0008)

5

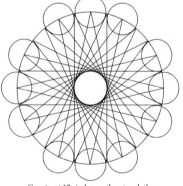

Construct 12 circles, so they touch the sides of adjacent heptagram arms.

6

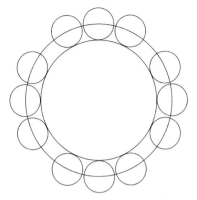

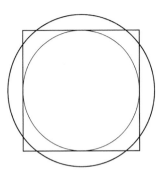

Remove 28 fold construction and inscribe a circle so that it touches 12 surrounding circles. **7**

Enclose this circle in a square. The original circle has now been squared. **8**

The Heavenly City

The modern world is obviously chaotic and unstable. Much of it is ruled by groups or individuals so ignorant that they do not even know there is such a thing as wisdom. To them and their followers this obscure incident in a corner of Wiltshire is laughably insignificant. They do not want to know about it, and least of all do they want to hear about the knowledge it conveys. That does not seem to matter to the unknown artists who are putting forth this knowledge. Year after year they continue their work in the summer cornfields, producing original designs, geometrically themed, which inevitably affect the minds of those who pay attention to them. This is communication on the highest level, far above the channelings of self-centred New Age mystics. It is the due and timely revelation of truths that are inseparable from human culture. We are privileged to be living in these times of signs and wonders, with freedom to enjoy them and learn from them. These may be the 'last days' - the end of one social and mental system and the beginning of another - but these times of transition, when former standards of culture and conduct no longer obtain, are the best times for individual pleasure. Plato remarked on that. In the last days, he said, you can do and think much as you like, and you meet the most remarkable people.

That is my experience today. Never before have we been so free, so comfortable, so uninhibited in following our own interests or admitting the influence of ancient gods into our minds. It will not last long, I know, but I can think of no better use for present freedom than to record and elucidate, in partnership with Allan Brown, the world-changing information that is encoded in the Crooked Soley crop circle.

The greater Soley circle

Obvious features of the Crooked Soley formation are the numbers 504 and 792 in its pattern, and its six-fold structure emphasized by the implied six-pointed star between its inner and outer rings (see fig 5). Other features are less apparent and only reveal themselves when the site of the formation is studied in greater depth.

A question that Allan Brown has looked into is why was the circle placed at that particular spot? He noticed that the site of the circle forms one point of a large equilateral triangle whose other points are at the respective centres of the two farm hamlets, Crooked Soley and Straight Soley (see fig 21). A circle drawn around this triangle has a diameter of some 4200 ft, which is 14 times the estimated 300 ft diameter of the crop circle.

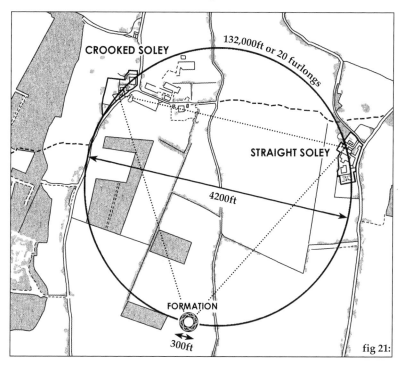

fig 21:

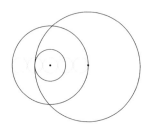

Construct 5 circles. A larger circle contains them, another circle passes through the centres of the two sizing circles, left & right of the centre. **1**

A circle with its centre on the circumference of the containing circle touches the smaller circle, which is $2/5^{\text{th}}$ the size of the containing circle. **2**

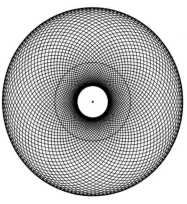

Rotate this circle about centre: 72 circles altogether. **3**

An equilateral triangle determines outer circumference of construction. **4**

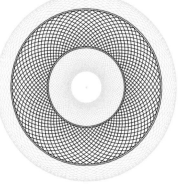

Pull circumferences in slightly to create the required parameters for the latticework field. **5**

Latticework field of 1296 divisions with inner & outer paths highlighted. **6**

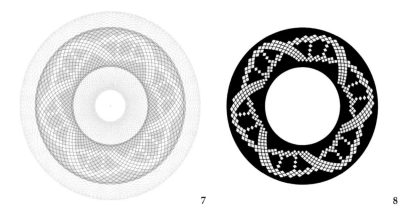

7   8

fig 23:

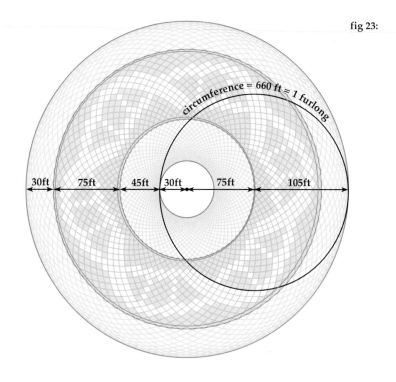

circumference = 660 ft = 1 furlong

| 30ft | 75ft | 45ft | 30ft | 75ft | 105ft |

The dimensions of the Crooked Soley formation

43

Moreover, when the complete pattern of the crop circle, with its 72 component circles, is raised to the scale of the large, landscape triangle and superimposed on it, the overall diameter of the greater figure is 5040 and its semi-circumference 7920 feet.

These two key numbers in the Crooked Soley design have metrological significance: they feature in the ancient, universal code of number from which all pre-metric units of measure were derived. The basic unit, in terms of which they are defined, is the traditional English foot (1 ft). Relating to it as 126:125 is the ancient Greek foot of 1.008 ft. Five thousand Greek feet make the Greek mile of 5040 ft. 7920 is inherent in English metrology because 7920 ft = a mile and a half or 12 furlongs.

A square with a side measuring 7920 ft contains 1440 acres or 12 hides of land (the legendary area granted to the 12 missionaries from the Holy Land, led by St. Joseph of Arimathaea, who founded Europe's first Christian settlement at Glastonbury).

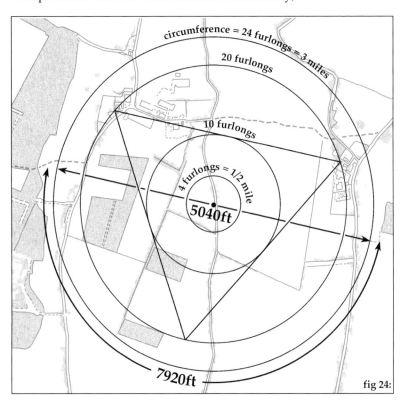

fig 24:

Figs 23 and 24 display the proportions and measures of the two circular designs discovered at Crooked Soley – the short lived circle and the greater circle, 14 times larger than the first, that appears on the map. In these the most prominent unit is the furlong of 660 ft, eight of which constitute a mile of 5280 ft. In the crop circle, each of the 72 circles in its construction has a radius of 105 ft and a circumference of 660 ft or 1 furlong. In the greater pattern the circumference of the outer circle is 3 miles or 24 furlongs, and each of the successive rings towards the centre is also measured in furlongs.

The 12 Hides of Glaston   **fig 25:**

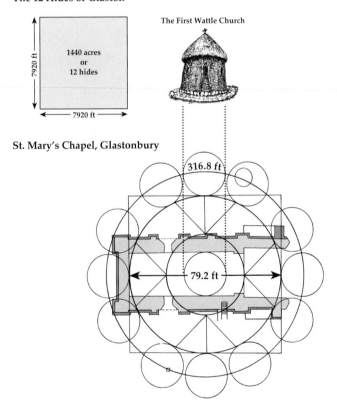

Diameter = 79.2 ft; perimeter of square = 316.8 ft; circumference of circle = 316.8 ft

St. Mary's Chapel, Glastonbury, on the site of the early Christian settlement. The cells of the original twelve missionaries at Glastonbury were placed around the central shrine in conformity with the proportions and numbers of the Heavenly City plan (see also fig 15).

45

The names behind the numbers

Arithmetic is a sacred science and its number is 504. That is because arithmetic is a Greek word, and in ancient Greek letters were symbols of both sounds and numbers. Each of the 24 letters in the alphabet corresponded to a number, ranging from 1 (alpha) to 800 (omega). These correspondances are set out below.

$A\ \alpha$	$B\ \beta$	$\Gamma\ \gamma$	$\varDelta\ \delta$	$E\ \varepsilon$	$Z\ \zeta$	$H\ \eta$	$\varTheta\ \theta$
1	2	3	4	5	7	8	9
$I\ \iota$	$K\ \varkappa$	$\varLambda\ \lambda$	$M\ \mu$	$N\ \nu$	$\varXi\ \xi$	$O\ o$	$\varPi\ \pi$
10	20	30	40	50	60	70	80
$P\ \varrho$	$\varSigma\ \sigma, \varsigma$	$T\ \tau$	$Y\ \upsilon$	$\varPhi\ \varphi$	$X\ \chi$	$\varPsi\ \psi$	$\varOmega\ \omega$
100	200	300	400	500	600	700	800

By adding together the eleven numbers corresponding to the eleven letters in αριθμετικα, arithmetic, the number obtained is 504. This mystical technique is called 'gematria'.

The art of deriving names from numbers is esoteric and magical. It was a science of initiates, in music, architecture and sacred writings. The initiated temple-builders wove spells and invocations into everything they created, using proportions and measures to encode a series of numbers, reflecting the characteristic numbers of the god or gods to whom each temple was dedicated.

The names of the gods, virtues and sacred principles were derived from the sounds by which they were invoked, and each sound had its own letter and number. These numbers together made up a 'pleroma' or totality, which was essentially a numerical expression of the universe and included all the harmonies, proportions and spiritual powers of which it is constructed. From it were obtained the music and ritual which sustained all ancient civilizations, and it was depicted as a geometrical, cosmological figure, the Heavenly Jerusalem of St John's vision, in which all shapes, colours and divine names are combined within the framework of perfect order which is the first attribute of Creation.

This science was widely known throughout the ancient world and accounts for the similarity of cultural traditions in every age and continent. That fact is unrecognised by modern scholars, because the tradition itself is no longer known. Even its very existence has been forgotten. The early Christians inherited it, together with the system of initiation through which it is kept alive, but from the second century onwards the esoteric tradition was suppressed by the Church. Also suppressed were the Gnostic teachers who had adapted pagan science to the cult of Jesus. Yet even the name of Jesus is a work of the Gnostic initiates who shaped Christianity. The number of that name (in the Greek of the New Testament) is 888, and it was constructed to bring out that number, for 888 is the number of the Founder.

Gematria of the Canonical circle fig 26:

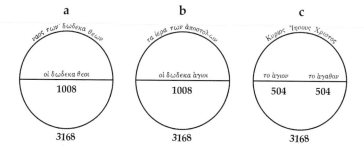

a Diameter: **The 12 Gods** *(1008)*
   Circumference: **Temple of the 12 Gods** *(3168)*

b Diameter: **The 12 Saints** *(1008)*
   Circumference: **The Sanctuaries of the Apostles** *(3168)*

c Radius (left): **The Holy** *(504)* Radius (right): **The Good** *(504)*
   Circumference: **Lord Jesus Christ** *(3168)*

All the sacred names of Christianity were constructed in the same way, to produce numbers that correspond to those of the sacred principles in earlier, pagan religions. In this system the Crooked Soley numbers, 504 and 792 are most prominent. Shown above are diagrams of the cosmological circle, radius 504 and circumference 4 x 792 or 3168. The last number, 3168, is the root of the supreme title in Christianity, **Κυριος Ιησους Χροστος**, Lord Jesus Christ, the letters in which add up to 3168. Other phrases of

47

which the Greek letters produce the number 3168 include the pagan 'Temple of the Twelve Gods' and the Christian adaptation, 'Shrines of the Apostles'. The transition from pagan to Christian terms is repeated in the diameter of the circle, the measure of which is 3168 divided by 22/7 or 1008. This is the number of 'the Twelve Gods' and 1008 is also the number of 'the Twelve Saints', a further reference to the apostles.

The radius of the circle, 504, has the number that represents the two highest principles in classical paganism, 'the Holy' and 'the Good'. Both these names in Greek produce 504. Another of the key numbers in the Crooked Soley formation, 720, implies Understanding or *nous*, meaning the enlightened state achieved through initiation.

Finally the numbers of divisions in the field at Crooked Soley is 1296, the sum of 504 and 792 and the product of 6 x 6 x 6 x 6. Six is the most perfect of numbers because its factors, 1 ,2, 3, produce 6 by both addition and multiplication. It is also called the marriage number. 1296, the fourfold six, must have a special meaning. It can be found in a name whose letters add up to 1296. That name is Goddess of All, Θεα Παντων.

To that great deity, paramount in nature, the wonderous creation at Crooked Soley is appropriately dedicated (see page 61).

John Michell

The pi pattern

Patterns containing the same numbers as the Crooked Soley crop formation can be simply generated in the following manner. The 1296 total grid 'square' count of the design, made up of 792 flattened and 504 standing 'squares', is laid out in an orthogonal grid of 36 by 36 squares. If a 1/36th part (ie. a 6 by 6 square) of the whole grid is taken, and 14 of the available 36 squares coloured in white and the remaining 22 squares left empty, you create a master square, which when multiplied out by a factor of 36 generates the numbers 792 and 504. We have titled this particular series of patterns the 'pi pattern' as it reflects the basic 22/7 pi approximation that figures throughout this work. The number 14 is intriguingly reiterated in this procedure, 14 being the factor through which the formation and the larger landscape circle are related.

The pi pattern grid: 36 x 36 = 1296 (6⁴)

6 x 6 = 36 (6²)

white = 14
black = <u>22</u>
6 x 6 = 36

14 x 36 = 504
22 x 36 = <u>792</u>
36 x 36 = 1296

54

white = 56
black = 88
12 x 12 = 144

56 x 9 = 504
88 x 9 = 792
144 x 9 = 1296

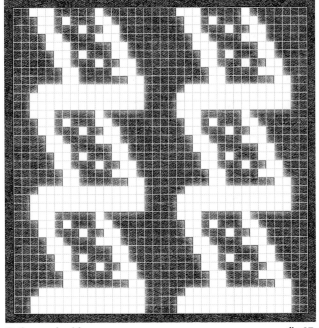

white = 84
black = 132
18 x 12 = 216

84 x 6 = 504
132 x 6 = 792
216 x 6 = 1296

Orthogonal grid - *square*   **fig 27:**

It is possible to reorganize the Crooked Soley design around the same basic pi-pattern grid. In order to create the motif the grid is broken down into six smaller units, each made up of an 18 by 12 rectangle. (18 x 12 = 216; 216 x 6 = 1296). Of these 216 squares, 84 are coloured white and the other 132 are left empty. The configuration differs slightly from the pi patterns shown previously, but the principle remains the same and the resulting numerology is identical.

If this square grid is cut vertically down the central axis and the two halves reconstituted as an 18 by 72 rectangle, the Crooked Soley design is returned to a single cohesive strand. Fig 29 shows what this strip would look like if it were bent back round into a circle so that its ends met. Although it fulfills the same numerical criteria as the original Crooked Soley design, it is clear that if the design is constructed over anything but this circular grid it loses its elegance and three dimensionality (see figs 29 & 30).

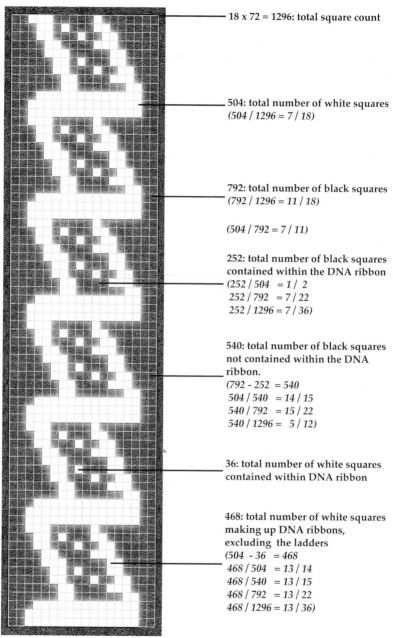

18 x 72 = 1296: total square count

504: total number of white squares
(504 / 1296 = 7 / 18)

792: total number of black squares
(792 / 1296 = 11 / 18)

(504 / 792 = 7 / 11)

252: total number of black squares
contained within the DNA ribbon
(252 / 504 = 1 / 2
252 / 792 = 7 / 22
252 / 1296 = 7 / 36)

540: total number of black squares
not contained within the DNA
ribbon.
(792 - 252 = 540
504 / 540 = 14 / 15
540 / 792 = 15 / 22
540 / 1296 = 5 / 12)

36: total number of white squares
contained within DNA ribbon

468: total number of white squares
making up DNA ribbons,
excluding the ladders
(504 - 36 = 468
468 / 504 = 13 / 14
468 / 540 = 13 / 15
468 / 792 = 13 / 22
468 / 1296 = 13 / 36)

Orthogonal grid - *rectilinear*

fig 28:

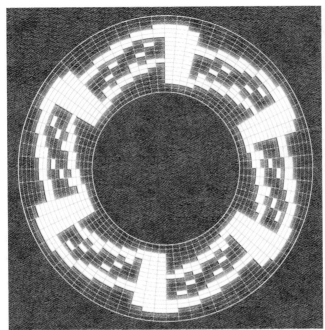

**Orthogonal
grid - *circular***

fig 29:

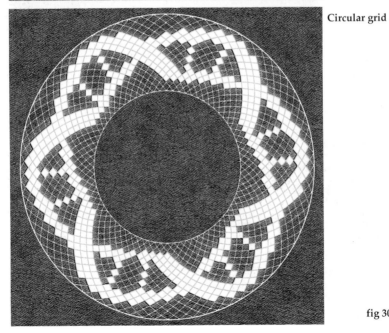

Circular grid

fig 30:

TO THE UNIVERSAL GODDESS

Θεα Παντω
1296

The dedication of the Crooked Soley circle is spelt out in the number of its divisions, **1296** = Θεα Παντων, the **Goddess of all Creation**

Mercurius in the cornfields

E very now and then, despite the attempts of the prevailing orthodoxies to suppress it, what the Neoplatonists called *Anima Mundi*, the Soul of the World, returns from its ancient exile. Crop circles are evidence of such a return.

Anima Mundi is like a vast storehouse of images which, combined in narrative action, we know as myths. Its nature is collective and impersonal, but it also manifests itself paradoxically in an individual and personal way, that is, as human souls. We participate in the Soul of the World inasmuch as we apprehend, express and enact its images and myths. In other words, the soul is the imaginative faculty in man.

The soul can never be known in itself; it can only be inferred from the images it spontaneously produces. One such image is the crop circle. From it we infer a whirling wind-like phenomenon which has left its imprint on the world. As the Holy Spirit, the soul is characterised as a wind - an invisible wind that bloweth whither it listeth. The native motion of the soul, according to Plotinus, is circular.

The world can be cut any way you like, but the inclination of Western culture has been to cut it in two: spirit and matter, mind and body, subject and object, God and Nature, sacred and secular and so on, it seems, forever. But the Platonic tradition describes a third realm, which neither Christianity nor science allow. This third realm, both mediating between the two halves of the world yet maintaining distinctions between them, is the realm of soul. It is neither spiritual nor material, neither inner nor outer, etc. but always ambiguous, always both-and. It is a 'subtle' or 'breath-body' which, Proteus-like, can take on any shape. Crop circles belong to this third realm.

Crop circles are both images within the soul and images of the soul. That is, they are symbols. As images within the soul, anything whatsoever can be a symbol; as images of the soul, all symbols are inexhaustible as to meaning. Like circles, symbols are both self-contained and self-transcending. Unlike signs or emblems, they can't be translated into another value or meaning; they are themselves meaning. Or they are the sum total of meaning that can be attached to or evoked by them. We cannot therefore say what crop circles mean; we can only say what they mean to us or what they are like.

Crop circles are like lacunae in the continuity of Nature; like windows on to the underworld; like holes through which we plummet to the depths; like obstacles, obstructions, obsessions on which our unimaginative functions stumble. They have to be approached in the same manner as they approach us - from the imagination. They are like a metaphorical vortex around which myths (stories, theories) circulate, but whose centre is empty, illimitable, undefinable. They are like the mirror Nature holds up to us. (His reflections are ugly and banal; hers are distorted and mad; mine, lucid and beautiful).

Crop circles are like the scars by which the Soul of the World initiates herself into the mystery of her own body, the Earth; yet they are also like the circular mandalas which, appearing at the crisis of a soul's distress, are (as C.G. Jung said) 'attempts at self-healing'. They are like dreams: to interrogate them is to force them to lie; to interpret them is to diminish their richness; to explain them is to misunderstand them. They are like messengers from the gods who notoriously do not want to be understood, but heeded. Crop circles are like mouths that speak to us of the strangeness and depth of things - speak to the heart more than the head and to the soul more than the heart. We only have to listen for God's sake.

Crop circles are also relations of UFOs. To grasp this, it is helpful to think Hermetically for a moment, like an alchemist. It is easy to see that UFOs come from the middle realm of soul. Their reality is a psychic one - that is, they are neither spirit (immaterial) nor body (material), but both. It is not so easy to see that crop circles are the same because their materiality blinds us to their spiritual dimension - until, of course, we go beneath the surface and find ourselves sucked out of our depth and into theirs. Paradoxes and contradictions are the hallmarks of psychic reality, and crop circles naturally generate their fair share of these.

Fundamental to alchemy were the twin operations of making 'that which is above like that which is below' and of making 'the volatile fixed and the fixed volatile'. Above/Below, volatile/fixed - these, along with such pairs as sun/moon, king/queen, soul/body etc. were the kind of perspectives through which the alchemists imagined the world. They are in fact the perspectives through which the soul prefers to imagine the world. Now oppositional, now complementary, the pairs permutated themselves in sets of analogies, like a kaleidoscope, in order to interpenetrate each other and to ravel each other up so that all might be reconciled in the one Stone. This is the operation that the Soul of the World is spontaneously enacting in front of our eyes. The volatile UFOs become fixed crop circles; that which was Above is made like that which is Below. Or, to put it another way, UFOs are to crop circles as volatile is to fixed as Above is to Below as air is to earth.

These archetypal perspectives work no less effectively, if less obviously, within the phenomenology of crop circles as well as the phenomena themselves. Thus all theories about UFOs or crop circles are myths which belong to a larger mythology and which are related to each other analogically. For example, the extraterrestrial hypothesis is to the earthlights hypothesis as Above is to Below. Both are true but neither should be taken literally. 'Earth energy', like 'plasma vortices', is a metaphor for the soul of the world (which is itself a metaphor for that reality about which we know nothing except that it forms images of and metaphors for itself).

The soul prefers to body itself forth - to imagine - in personifications. The Neoplatonists call these daimons. They are neither gods nor physical humans but inhabitants of the middle realm - nymphs, satyrs, djinns, trolls, fairies, angels etc. Unlike the transcendent gods who belong to spirit not soul, they are immanent in the world, whether on earth, just below its surface or just above it. Eros is a daimon. As Plato has Diotima say in the *Symposium*: 'Everything that is daimonic is intermediate between God and mortal. Interpreting and conveying the wishes of men to Gods and the will of Gods to men, it stands between the two and fills the gap... God has no contact with man; only through the daimonic is there intercourse and conversation between men and Gods, whether in the waking state or during sleep.'

Crop circles are daimonic; and, since the daimons prefer to appear as persons, we may expect personifications of crop circles - possibly fairies or 'mowing devils' or, more likely, imps like Robin Goodfellow[1].

To say that such daimons cause crop circles says more about the way we think. Daimons tend to disregard causality just as they ignore other laws, such as space and time, that we are pleased to impose on a world whose reality is quite otherwise. Analogously, we think of alien entities as directing or occupying UFOs. It may be that they are alternative manifestations - personifications - of UFOs. I have mentioned elsewhere[2] how Napoleon had a familiar spirit 'which protected him, guided him, as a daimon, and which at particular moments took on the shape of a shining sphere, which he called his star, or which visited him in the figure of a dwarf clothed in red that warned him.'[3] A thorough going description of daimons can be found in Iamblichus.[4] Those with attributes of rapidity, luminosity, elusiveness etc should be of particular interest to ufologists and proponents of 'plasma vortex' theories.

Plutarch warns[5] that he who denies the daimons breaks the chain that unites the world to God. Christianity, science and philosophy have all denied the daimons. Worse, they have demonised them. But, kick a daimon out of the front door and it returns by the back. Christianity tried to dogmatise Christ as the sole mediator between man and God, but the daimons returned disguised as cults of the Virgin Mary and the saints. With the decline of Christianity, the daimons return more boldly and in their former pre-eminent position, for instance, as things seen in the skies. In philosophy they return as a pandemonium of abstract concepts and essences; in science they pop up as a phantasmagoria of quasars and quarks and plasma vortices.

In psychology the outlawed daimons return as moods. For to attack the realm of soul is to attack the *anima* who personifies, aestheticizes, keeps us in relation to Nature and to each other, prevents us from pursuing too ardently those transcendental truths of science and ideology which would set themselves up as absolutes. Crop circles are instinct with anima. They are capricious, flighty and seductive; they insist on ambiguity and mystery. They offer a mute rebuke to those brutalised by that unreasonable excess of rationality which demands explanations, definitions, order at all costs and so denies anima. She returns, naturally, from behind, from below, as irritability and petulance, resentment and spite; she seeps up through all our attempts to think logically and clearly, muddying them, dragging them down, poisoning them. In casting out the daimons from our writing, we let in the demons.

The only way to get rid of anima is to bore her. In this case she manifests herself as absence, as loss of soul - in the dead mechanical language of theorists who are bent on defining and categorising what cannot be treated in this way. As specimens are killed before they are subjected to the microscope, so this type of theorist murders whatever of wonder there is in crop circles and replaces it with detailed classifications. But there can be no technical manual of crop circles. What look like hard facts are soft, if indeed they are facts at all. Crop circles are not problems to be solved but mysteries to be entered, like labyrinths. The language appropriate to them is the language of myth. 'It is not possible to speak rightly about the gods without the gods.' (Iamblichus.)

As Plotinus said, the 'configurations of the soul need containers.' Specifically he meant altars, shrines, statues, vessels, in which the daimonic can find comfortable expression. Tumuli, stone circles, circular graveyards are such shrines as, perhaps, is this book. The iconoclasm of the age has deprived the daimons of their proper places of recognition and so they crop up in the very realm from which they have been banished: Nature. Crop circles are their own shrines.

The debate concerning the relationship of the daimons to the gods is a perplexed one which I won't rehearse here. I like Proclus's idea[6]: '...about every god there is an innumerable multitude of daimons, who have the same appellations with their leaders... because they express in themselves the characteristic peculiarity of their leading god.'

Thus the daimons are like the preceding retinue of the greater gods. Which deity is behind crop circles? Pan perhaps; or Demeter, goddess of fields and growing crops; or Gaia who guards the earth just below Demeter's domain and is the goddess of place and of the rituals that generate fertility[7]. However, the deities never come alone (unless their nature is to be monomaniac like Zeus or Jehovah). They are related to each other by blood or marriage. Both Gaia and Demeter are linked to the inhuman mineral depths of the earth, the former through *chthon* - that shadowy quasi-deity who signifies the depths, the world of the dead (Gaia-chthonia was worshipped on Mykonos) - and the latter through her daughter Persephone who was abducted by Hades. Crop circles are daimonic zones where Demeter-Gaia-chthon overlap. The green womb of Dame Kind leads to the blackness of death. Yet, as solar circles on the golden corn, crop circles are also the point at which the sky god Apollo presses lovingly down on mother Earth, foreshadowing the marriage of Heaven and Earth. Thus crop circles connect the depths to the surface and the surface to the heights; they are symbols of middle earth, mediating between the sky world and the underworld.

Wherever we meet anomalies we know that Hermes is not far away. He is the most daimonic of the gods because he is their messenger, scurrying on winged sandals to and fro between transcendent Olympus and the world of man. He is the particular thorn in the side of the god of science - Apollo, who loses his masculine detachment, clarity, sense of formal beauty and purity of purpose when Hermes steals (and possibly mutilates) his cattle. Hermes is also god of borders and crossroads where the ways, vertical as well as horizontal, meet; piles of stones or herms mark the sacred spots where he has trodden. Crop circles are like herms.

The nature of Hermes is given new dimensions by his Latin counterpart, Mercurius, god of alchemy and Hermetic philosophy[8]. Mercurius is both earth spirit and soul of the world, volatile and fixed, Above and Below, psychic and hylic. He is a trickster, either harmlessly impish or seriously diabolical. His handiwork can be discerned in crop circles which tease us into pursuing him while he maddens us by remaining always just out of reach.

Mercurius is the god of hoaxes. A hoax aims to expose some flaw in society. If I pass myself off as a social worker and ask to examine people's children, this can be both comic and moral - for example, as a satire on a society which has become depersonalised, allowing bureaucracy to hinder right relationships. If I proceed to harm those children, the hoax becomes criminal and even diabolical. There is a sinister aspect to all tricksters: they like to play god, or the devil, behind the scenes.

Crop circles are like hoaxes in that they expose our wrong relationship to Nature and mock our methods of investigation. In the end, it may not matter if the hoax is perpetrated directly by Mercurius or through the agency of human hoaxers.

Another kind of hoax is the practical joke. It is aimed not at society but at the individual, with the intention of de-intoxicating him from his illusions. In comedy, practical jokes bring self-knowledge to those who have a fantastic idea of themselves. Practical jokers have to unmask themselves in the end and their satisfaction is in seeing the look on the faces of the duped who thought they were acting freely but were really being manipulated all along by the joker.

But what of the joker who does not unmask, like the perpetrator of crop circles? He forces us to unmask ourselves. He needs no satisfaction from the look on our faces. He manipulates for its own sake. He knows us better than we know ourselves. He wants to deflate our self-importance, undermine our principles and beliefs, threaten our reason. He is invisible, ruthless and impersonal, like a psychopath or a god. He is Mercurius who, like Lucifer, both deceives in order to destroy and deceives in order to bring light. If we do not know ourselves, that is, know, discern, listen to our daimons - and demons - we are easy prey for the darker side of Mercurius. Let us pray that his tricks stop at crop circles.

Patrick Harpur

NOTES

1. See *Fortean Times*, No#53, p48.
2. See 'Imaginary Reality' in *Magonia*, No.32.
3. Quoted in Jaffé, Aniela. *Apparitions* (Univ.of Dallas, 1978).
4. See *On the Mysteries of the Egyptians,
    Chaldeans, and Assyrians*. Trans. T. Taylor (1821).
5. In *De Defectu Oraculorum*, 13.
6. In his *First Alcibiades* commentary.
7. See Hillman, James. *The Dream and the Underworld* (Harper and Row, 1979).
8. See Harpur, Patrick (ed.). *Mercurius, or the
    Marriage of Heaven and Earth* (Macmillan, 1990).

(First published in THE CEREOLOGIST, number 1 – Summer of 1990)

A caution to readers

The crop circle phenomenon is wondrous and inspirational, and it is also dangerously powerful. To many people it has brought a new interest in life, but others have been upset and disillusioned by the trickery surrounding it or by its failure to develop according to their expectations. For better or worse, crop circles are highly addictive.

Like all addictions, crop circles are not helpful in your career. One addict I met, an American writer on crop circles, said that he had sacrificed a lavish income by devoting himself to crop circle studies. And he is not the only one. Many of the original researchers, veterans from the 1980s, have left the subject but still retain the addict's fascination for it. We, the authors of this monograph, are clearly addicted. We have spent a lot of time on crop circles and related phenomena - with nothing material to show for it. We cannot conscientiously advise anyone to enter the murky world of crop circle research.

If you choose to do so - at your own risk, of course - you enter a world of magic. No one has ever spent a summer in the ancient, sacred heart of England, from Avebury to the Vale of Pewsey, where the light and atmosphere are intense and crop circles proliferate, without being changed by the experience. You meet the most remarkable people, and you partake in a process whereby the light of divine knowledge enters minds, and hearts are stirred by the beauty of crop circles in their chosen setting. If you need an addiction, this is the best one you could find. We call it dedication - to the ideals of justice and true proportion and the restoration of divine rule on earth.

John Michell

Index

Bibliography

Daimonic Reality: A Field Guide to the Otherworld, Patrick Harpur, Pine Winds Press, 2003

Mercurius: or the Marriage of Heaven and Earth, Patrick Harpur, Macmillan, 1990

The Philosophers' Secret Fire: A History of the Imagination, Patrick Harpur, Ivan R. Dee, 2003

Ancient Metrology, John Michell, Pentacle Books, 1981

At the Centre of the World, John Michell, Thames & Hudson, 1994

City of Revelation, John Michell, Garnstone Press, 1972

New Light on the Ancient Mystery of Glastonbury, John Michell, Gothic Image Publications, 1990

The Dimensions of Paradise: The Proportions and Symbolic Numbers of Ancient Cosmology, John Michell, Adventures Unlimited Press, 2001

The Face and the Message: What do they mean and where are they from? John Michell, Gothic Image Publications, 2002

The New View Over Atlantis, John Michell, Thames & Hudson, 1983

Twelve Tribe Nations and the Science of Enchanting the Landscape, John Michell & Christine Rhone, Thames & Hudson, 1991

Crop Circles, Michael Glickman, Wooden Books, 2005

All Done With Mirrors, John Neal, The Secret Academy, 2000

Crop circles: selected reading (A - Z by authors)

Crop Circle Year Books, Steve Alexander & Karen Douglas, Temporary Temple Press 1999 onwards, 28pp

Phanomen Kornkreise, Werner Anderhub & Andreas Müller, AT-Verlag, Baden 2005, 128 pp

Crop Circles: Exploring the Designs & Mysteries, Werner Anderhub & Hans Peter Roth, Lark Books, 2002, 144pp

Crop Circles: Harbingers of World Change, ed. Alick Bartholomew, Gateway 1991, 192pp

Ciphers in the Crops, ed. Beth Davis, Gateway 1992, 88pp

Circular Evidence, Pat Delgado & Colin Andrews, Bloomsbury 1989, 190pp

Crop Circles, Michael Glickman, Wooden Books 2005, 58pp

The Deepening Complexity of Crop Circles, Dr Eltjo Haselhoff, Frog Ltd. 2001, 157pp

The Cosmic Connection, Michael Hesemann, Gateway 1996, 168pp

Mysterious Lights and Crop Circles, Linda Moulton Howe, Paper Chase Press 2000, 342pp

Crop Circles: The Hidden Form, Nick Kollerstrom, Wessex Books 2002, 64pp

Crop Circle Geometry, John Martineau, Wooden Books 1992 onwards, varied pages

The Circles Effect and its Mysteries, George Terence Meaden, Artetech 1989, 116pp

The Face & the Message, John Michell, Gothic Image 2002, 36pp

Crop Circles Revealed, Judith Moore and Barbara Lamb, Light Technology Publishing 2001, 265pp

The Crop Circle Enigma, ed. Ralph Noyes, Gateway 1990, 192pp

Crop Circles: The Greatest Mystery of Modern Times, Lucy Pringle, Thorsons 1999, 144p

Round in Circles, Jim Schnabel, Penguin 1993, 295pp

Secrets in the Fields, Freddy Silva, Hampton Roads 2002, 334pp

Fields of Mystery, Andy Thomas, S B Publications 1996, 100pp

Quest for Contact, Andy Thomas & Paul Bura, S B Publications 1997, 144pp

Vital Signs: A Complete Guide to the Crop Circle Mystery and Why it is NOT a Hoax, Andy Thomas, S B Publications (Frog Ltd in USA) 1998, revised 2002, 192pp

Swirled Harvest, Andy Thomas, Vital Signs Publishing & S B Publications 2003, 176pp

An Introduction to Crop Circles, ed. Andy Thomas, Wessex Books 2003, 48pp

The Secret History of Crop Circles, Terry Wilson, CCCS 1998, 155pp

Selected crop circle websites (A - Z by title)

BLT RESEARCH: http://www.bltresearch.com

CIRCLEMAKERS: http://www.circlemakers.org

CROP CIRCLE CONNECTOR: http://www.cropcircleconnector.com

CROP CIRCLE NEWS: http://www.cropcirclenews.com

CROP CIRCLE RESEARCH: http://www.cropcircleresearch.com

DAVID KINGSTON: http://www.thecropcirclewebsite.50megs.com

JONAH OHAYV: http://www.korncirkler.dk

KORNKREISE-FORSCHUNG: http://www.kornkreise-forschung.de

LUCY PRINGLE: http://www.lucypringle.co.uk

MICHAEL GLICKMAN: http://www.michaelglickman.net

SWIRLED NEWS: http://www.swirlednews.com

TEMPORARY TEMPLES: http://www.temporarytemples.co.uk

UK CROP CIRCLES: http://www.ukcropcircles.co.uk